# THE CALFBEARER

T0099375

# The Calfbearer

Ida Affleck Graves

OXFORD
UNIVERSITY PRESS

*Oxford University Press, Great Clarendon Street, Oxford* OX2 6DP

*Oxford New York*

*Athens Auckland Bangkok Bogotá Buenos Aires Calcutta
Cape Town Chennai Dar es Salaam Delhi Florence Hong Kong Istanbul
Karachi Kuala Lumpur Madrid Melbourne Mexico City Mumbai
Nairobi Paris São Paulo Singapore Taipei Tokyo Toronto Warsaw*

*and associated companies in Berlin Ibadan*

*Oxford is a registered trade mark of Oxford University Press*

*Published in the United States
by Oxford University Press Inc., New York*

*First published in Oxford Poets
as an Oxford University Press paperback 1999*

*British Library Cataloguing in Publication Data
Data available*

*Library of Congress Cataloging in Publication Data
Data available*

*ISBN 1–19–288110–8*

1 3 5 7 9 10 8 6 4 2

*Typeset by George Hammond Design
Printed in Great Britain by
Athenæum Press Ltd.
Gateshead, Tyne and Wear*

PETER WALLIS
THANK YOU

# Acknowledgements

Most of these poems were written since *A Kind Husband* of 1994. A few have been previously published, and thanks are due to the editors of *The Rialto*, *Samphire*, the *Aldeburgh Poetry Festival Catalogue 1997*, and to the BBC Radio 4 'Woman's Hour'.

# Contents

The Calfbearer   1
A Death   2
A Balloon   3
A Skeleton   4
Chocs   5
A Favour   6
A Wedding   7
Station Platform   8
Fog   8
The Trunk   9
A Fever   10
Sitting on the Stairs   11
A Welcome   12
Lamb Chop   13
A Bathing Hut   14
A Prince   15
Sums   16
Tapioca   17
Loot   18
A High Window   19
A Cushion   20
Snails   21
A Rag Doll   22
Thrush   23
A Velvet Bonnet   24
A Shock   25
Message in a Bottle   26
Bed-fellow   27
Young Girl of Clacton   28
A Lover   29

Recorded Delivery  30
Wrong Number  31
A Bench  32
The Caravan  33
Chain Smoker  34
Faces  35
The Deck Chair  36
Encounter  37
Sell-by Date  38
A Linen Line  39
Man and Wheelbarrow  40
Hanging Up Washing  41
Dandelion  42
A Weed  43
A Champagne Cork  44
Egg  45
Mouse  46
Tail on Fire  47
Cat Nut  48
Two Dogs  49
A Cow  50
Sheep  51
A Goat  51
A Hen  52
Red-Leg  53
Albino Bird  54
Walking By  55
Old Lady  56
Adam  57
Death of Adam  58
God  59
Satan  60
A Grave  61
A Long Farewell  62

# The Calfbearer

*(Athens, Acropolis Museum, 560 BC)*

Newborn, fresh licked, still slobbering,
I lift this calf and drape it, a warm scarf,
About me, neck shoulders, around my need for loving.
I bunch the infant bull hooves, my greed for him,
In one knotted clasp, in my two fists, in no doubt,
My wide elbows the structure of our unity, our debt.
Our faces side by side, close, calf gaze milky with content.
So what now my little god bull, my burden,
This to be a statue, shrine, an idea, gift, glory.
My heart gives it all to you, to lovers, to any,
All to everyone.

# A Death

In Poona our India, in hell's heat, in breathless swoon,
In a dim room, an outhouse, all forgotten.
A crack for comfort for a slim snake, a sleeping rat.
This is where, babe brother, one may weep alone,
May lie forlorn, blub, cry, bite one's knuckles,
Utter squeals, mouth wide, tongue flat, tense in despair.
This is the right and rich cry place to mourn for him.

Here now window slats, wire mesh, defy the sun's glare,
Boy Punka Wallah cools air, cord to a big toe.
On Mama's bed, under a white mist, a net, is a dead thing.
Some days ago we played Clap Hands, Ring-a-Roses, Peep-Bo.
I want to, long to weep, to holler to honour him
In that mucky, that glorious crying place. But I am done for,
Am dizzy with tears, tired. I adore him still,
But will mop up, will whisper to and rock my doll.

# A Balloon

That balloon there blots the blue, shocks the blue air,
Blots out breath from the heart, heart in a terror's fist,
Dares give the body blow to air, sky, to my infant chest.

My tongue tip in this terror implores the gap there
Where the milk tooth bit on doubt, was fretted out with a twist,
Lip and lung stiffen the throat's impossible swallow.

Sudden, the chance look up, this blot, balloon, snare
Dangles huge there, my tongue tells the escape out,
Moistens the yell, the howl, all silence clenched in it.

I stumble up, panic and weep up steps to a blind house,
I strive to knock, knock, the knocker too high up there,
Who to hear, hide, save me. No and nobody.
I slide sitting to find my tall self somewhere.

# A Skeleton

My Doc Dad in this attic reads with me beside,
Fingers spread long and pale on page, how amazing.
I touch him lightly, made curious by this idea's dazzling.
I am six years and may demand how come such shape and motion.
No reply. Then a chair fronting the corner curtain for my standing.
Rattle in tin trunk, out come somebody's bones all neatly wired.
Up it goes hooked and dangling. I clack the smile in the jawbone,
Intone a forlorn ditty. Caress the head, the finger, thumb, toe.
I play till dark and the moon lights white on this person.
Oh Skeleton, I shall have nothing now to fear, nor when stark alone.

## Chocs

My Ma's admirer aims to snare and stupefy her
With chocs, a tray display breaking her dense denials.
Her ringed fingers flutter a little, her breath tense,
Toes tighten a little in the spike-heeled fantasy.
Choose one. And two, three, five. Eyes shut to the yielding.
A *puff truffle*, *kissa noisette*, *rum fourré*, *fudge*,
And *marzipan*, *amande*, *mélange amor*, all four all nine.
They vanish. Their absence bewildering, oh strange subtle.
My Mama do not leave me. Or I die, and I die evermore.

# A Favour

A Colonel man, Mama's glad sweetheart man; but not mine,
Mine is oddly in and out, flash and gone, not fun.
This one chimes the rope bell for violets,
Hansom cabs, wine and glasses, tips golden money.

Ma begs a favour smiling a powdered bare shoulder,
Her indrawn breath grappling, clenching the corset, hooks, claws.
Ready. He balances, right foot braces against the round buttock,
Pulls, tightens, tugs the laces, ties. He and I both so adore her.

# A Wedding

Curtains on clatter rings mean those ding-dong weddings.
In boarding-house below the old munch cabbage, Ma sings.
Being small we wobble on chairs to tug, claw them off the rungs.

Pattern smothering us of dead leaves, daffs, buds and
      raspberries will do.
My chum yells in the lodger's big bowler, he wriggles No.
But I show off my brass furrel ring shouting I hate you so.

Fronting the flowery chamber pot, jug and basin,
We wed 'Oh I do, I do,' to prince nothing for ever and
      for every reason,
Trailing, tripping, wrapped in the curtains of every season.

My Ma, my Dadda drift silent, lonely and boneless instead,
Mum under a pink eiderdown, Dad on smelly attic bed.
When grown I might do ditto because it may not be so bad.

# Station Platform

I curdled. I am clenched cold, my small soul undone and utterly.
Yes, I am rigid with dread of it, that iron far railway engine.

I must be good, a good girl oh yes, she says or she will leave me.
Woe, nowhere and lost, no party dress, no sun merry air to tread on.

The shining rails, wide then narrowing with my sobs' terror
To a threat blot, a tunnel, the rush roar of my ribs' collapse.

This time this high-shrieking vast engine-thrust now defies me,
But I live, and pistons, the triple clatter
Rave savagely past and beyond me.


# Fog

A dense dirty smog, puffer train in a strange land, waiting.
My breath slain, punched, fright locked, hands wide oh save me.
My shoes in space, terror tears, my muff on a cord no comfort.
The station hissing, the window glass smudges of shapes passing.
My Mama a blur blot opposite, not loving, huge hat a smother.
Choking air but no air, I whimper. Her bulk moves, her voice
A scolding mutter 'Hush up now, no fuss; a nothing fog,
Not a good girl. Or will leave you, go, Not come back.'
Oh god I implore you. I bawl, yell, bellow, please oh.
The door slams. Smell of oily engine, a roar. Nobody opposite.
The whistle blows. Who or what comes in and sits is no matter.

# The Trunk

I watch. My Mama catches her breath with a wild sob.
Meaning me, weeping 'Oh my baby, poor babe, my child.'
Her hair long, lavish, irritates an eye and her naked thighs.
Yes, she kneels bent over a black leather trunk, wailing.
Yes, she is going. The lid raised she pats, folds a silky robe,
A petticoat, a chemise. Gazes, lays them back in again.
Who will give me milk, a sponge, a good-night slow kiss.
Her beaded kid shoes ready. In a round box her hat stabbed
     with a pin.
Oh woe, oh so soon she is going, I to grow undone  by this.

# A Fever

A fever, my leaden tousled head stabs hot and clammy.
Call doctor. The black bag, pin-stripe, hair parted in the middle.
This daft child only the cover-up, the dummy emergency.
His eye shines on the sly edge of Mum's petticoat.
Doc tyke mocks me   'She is his chick-a-biddie, his pretty chum'.
I wail. I chafe the pillow to divert their slippery fun.
He smiles 'When grown, I shall be his bride in an open boat afloat'.
There is a drill hid up my sleeve, hole in that hull.
I coax, I inflame our bridal fever riddle.
He steadies the pink spicy dose, intones 'Wider. Now open wide'.

# Sitting on the Stairs

A loose milk tooth, and that moon wedged in it to bite on,
This sudden Boarding-house, no ayah, horse-gari rides, no sun.

My knees to chin in night flannel, bosom double promise,
The moon too swells bulging terror deep to my distress.

Bulging huge, slow, slowly, flaming full on window glass,
A last smash-in, gone  all sky, air, all is my smothered life loss.

Stair lino cold, broken, danger stairs drop to a maimed piano,
Mum's song shrilling to a final high, roar and flow of their
        clapping.

My curl-rags too tight, she forgot milk biscuit, the smack kiss.
I saw that limp dog by door, tomorrow I will pat it.

# A Welcome

I arrive. They grip me out and over the step-gap.
The train pants, I stumble. They mean me to stay,
To live here. Cousins, grandpapa with his pet,
His mongrel pup, to meet me. I carry a heap.

Pup snarls at my sandals, snaps, leaps up.
My cousins slap each other, pull flip faces
Jump and ass about. Then race and collide up a hill.
They stop, giggling, quiet by a posh toy shop.

Grandpa grumpy. I long to collapse and cry.
He chooses, buys each a doll, wig, flop eyes, a frill.
For me nothing. I drip misery tears. But in my hold-all
I have knitted him a gold tie and presents for all.

# Lamb Chop

My small cousins have guzzled theirs, greens and all,
Each leaving a chewed bone and its paper frill.

Me, I am from a far land, a grey sea, on a growling boat
Here chattering white apes are all that I am not.

Oh my moist lamb chop I love you, how lovely you are,
Soon I will praise you with my new teeth but fear to tear.

Our grandpapa with doom in a glittering fork,
Stabs it, hurls it into the can of left-over muck,

And with it all love hugs kisses and the pale sunshine,
What I am here for, and once thought was mine.

# A Bathing Hut

I am Neptune's imp in this seaside hullabaloo,
I twist dry my musty damp bathing togs.
Now the big wheels start up, are rumbling on pebbles.
I listen for the horse jolting me to the water's edge,
I balance on the drainage, the wet floor slats and stink.
When I am grown, and soon, I shall not fear this jolt,
      this tumble shock
Shall soon close hug Neptune in my blue party frock
And give birth to twenty paddling pigs.

# A Prince

Here grass is trampled mud, is a dud crab apple,
Is three battered fences, shaky steps, the deep basement gloom,
A sky damping, throttling us all, a school huddle.

Think away my serge gym tunic, tickly bloomers,
Skimpy limp pigtail, spot on chin. Behold here I come,
A miraculous prince, high-kicker, whirling dance in every limb.

Our bum teacher sends message 'Nothing to laugh at.
That duffer. Stop it. Tell her to stop showing off.'
The prince totters stiffly. Is dead. The dagger bleeds red.
Sweet prince, I shall invite you to my wedding.

# Sums

I am flung on floor, door locked, forgotten.
Flies wobble dizzily up the window pane,
Tumble, whirl, wipe dusty eyes, climb again.
My cheek icy on lino like a stale kiss,
Like teacher's peck of dry goodbye.
My shins hit the stairs, she smacked, tossed me here.
No supper. I giggle, gaze at flies, at nothing.
And why. I cannot add, subtract, multiply,
Tell rich lies. But I will bewitch you with another,
With a wonder story of a dragon, a prince, a lover.
A fly falls, strives again, climbs steadily.

# *Tapioca*

Tapioca pud, oh no. Cannot munch up these mock eggs
Maybe writhing into a cluster of maggots with pin eyes,
Into undulating live horrors.
I will not eat. My behind sore with my sighs,
Agony of pricks and shivers in dangling legs.
Must sit here till I eat it all up, till I die.

When grown I will skip on chippings where my teacher lies,
I will strip my clothes off and blow raspberries,
I will not, no never, kiss a cross, a slobbery, or hairy face,
Nor wed a boss with sagging cash pockets,
I shall swear, stuff creamy cakes, pick locks,
I will not kneel down cold in any holy place,
Have a hat with sucked elastic under my chin.
I do refuse to say sorry when I did no sin.
The last bell clangs. I am weary, pants wet with weeping,
I lay my head down sideways and slide into sleep.

## Loot

A laugh, hiccup; a gulp, two hiccups and the rumbles.
Hungry, my chums and I, our tums in woe, finger fidgets.
So a trip-up down and down to the damp dark pantry.
I double my bed and night gowns corded for loot,
For bread and scraps high piled early, dim with flies.
Teachers chatter munch supper beyond doors. But danger,
I snatch, stuff the loved slices to chest, knics, waist,
Stumble, wobble laden up to hoorays, smiles, their kisses.
Now balance loot tenderly on top of hissing gas globe.
The marge melting, foul-smelling, and chew it, hushed, sober.

# A High Window

Sit beside her, by teacher, dinner-time while I tease it,
Do chum, while I scoop, slide it, plate to bag to pocket,
Cupped hand on fat slippery rancid mutton grease.
Must vanish it. So smirk, smile, flatter her do, my chum,
The boss bosom, gold watch on brooch, she won't notice.
My throat spews it, toes curl and tighten. No, will not eat it.
My new gym tunic gorged with fat comic in pocket,
Flaps heavy on scratchy knickers. Must get rid of it.

The change bell clangs. Breath smacked, I dash up,
Rush up and up the flight stairs, here the high window.
Chum, hold my legs, will lean out far, fling it far.
Her grip feeble. Fat scatters below. My eyes, my life
Follows in air.

# A Cushion

Girl-children, bored flat, in bedridden sick-bay,
Have spots, the weeps, tickle trouble fevers,
One says Tell. I rear up, sit, chin on knees,
Speak The Princess, Her Frog Lover, and Spells.
Then my silly An Apple, Elephant, and A Loud Sneeze.
They gurgle, giggle, strive to sit, scratch,
Rave out laughing, laugh to a collapse.
Laughing I trickle, wet, let go. Oh woe.
I snatch the red bed cushion, stuff it under, forget it.

Scarlet dye spread, soaked, is staining under and over.
Will get the pie-jaw for this, in corner, no supper.
Fifty lines, hang head crawling sorrow. Oh bother.
Chums save me acid drops, choc ice creams,
All their loves and lollipops.

# Snails

This girl-child idles by the Tell a True Story tree,
Is solitary. Child and chums once hiding from school hours
Balancing on boughs, no fibs, no sly cheating,
Told by turns, fables of Pa, Mama, of next-doors,
Some holy, soppy, peculiar. All odd and a tussle.
Why take the wine bottle up to bed with them,
With squeals, giggles, toss turning in wed rhythm,
Sometimes sobs. This teasing the tiresome puzzle.

The girl-child gazes down, two snails
Are writing entwined, eyes waving on stalks,
Slithering, sliding, slimed into one.
Girl stamps. Stamps and stamps on them. And again.
My memory now a ruin, heart's pain, violent, forever.

# A Rag Doll

The girl sits crumpled, crying, collapsed,
Her striped school tie twisted askew,
Her nails bitten. No need to have been so soft soppy.
The rag doll in shreds, a goner, tossed on cracked lino,
A rubbish. No head, stuffing burst out of its tum,
A sad stump of a neck and a red left leg,
The lost head button-eyed weeping somewhere.

Why so. She stood soppy, tranced, hushing the rag doll.
On a sudden we squealed, yelped, caught a hand,
And another. Leapt in a circle round her in a frenzy,
Laughter, in death dance. We tore at her darling.
Got it, mauled it, pulled it like crazy. Killed it.
I kneel, kneel now and always to Whoever, Whatever
Pleading. The rags murmur 'No' and 'No, not. Never.'

# *Thrush*

I climb the spiked railings at five o'clock mirky dawn.
I am nine, school naughty, idle, I will be a conqueror soon.
I spy a thrush toe-dancing for worms, for morning fun,
A speckled thrush tilting her eyes one side to the other.
Softly, slowly, not to disquiet her, I lie on grass. I am hers
    wholely.
By frail chance our gaze mingles one with another, held steadily.
Now thrush fluffs up feathers, spreads, arches wings in a wide
    curve
And crouches slowly low. So bewitched, she is all mine and rigid
    with love.
Now my hand may grip her, clutch, conquer her, my high power
    to prove.
Thrush, oh no and no. I adore, sigh for you. I clap, you move and
    off you fly.

# A Velvet Bonnet

Our teacher slaves for a pale curate,
We draw his angel mug for jokes on a slate.
She adores the upturned soles of his worn shoes,
She longs, listens to his Resurrection news,
She prays too asking mercy for his few flaws,
And pleads with her cup's tea-leaves for the Yes or No.
In a locked bedroom she bends over a toenail,
We squint through a keyhole seeing a scarlet glow.
While she eats we pinch the book from under her pillow,
For we have heard it is too rich rude to swallow.
My mum's new lover bought me a rare thing,
A bonnet, velvet, black with a red lining.
Our teacher dragged me by the neck down to the dustbin,
Made me clatter it in, said it was the most abominable sin.

# A Shock

A long box, a knotted, a narrow, a nameless one.
Not likely to be chocs, not candy, nor cookies
In paper fluted frills. Nor a dice game for our fun.
It lies delicious on my school dormie pillow,
Unstamped, unposted. 'You lucky sod, oh open it' a chum sighs.

Then the box tussle, tissue whispering a soft hurrah,
Of a heartbeat, of Cupid aiming a love arrow.
A shock. I am in shock, unable to speak, to swallow,
To see straight, hit in the tum, shattered, dumb.
A corset. Captivity with bones and laces. The start of glum tears,
A prison. The end of my dancing years.

# Message in a Bottle

Fun scribble to an unknown far dolt or heart-beat
Wide-flung dropt to water, fool slung far out, rocking
From cork to glass, my message, high and low on wave
     churning,
Twist of paper, bottle's knock on a wreck,
Swirl and drag to who knows where.

Maybe with litter trash, tossed dry on tar, tins, burning pebble.
Or maybe collides with a skinny tanned lad, shock high diving
For pearl. But only a bottle dull to a tight knuckle.
Uncork, name, number. Spill, spell out all my kisses,
Scatter them everywhere.

## Bed-Fellow

Opposite and too close, filthy and useless, that rag doll.
Neck frill to a crescent smile and a wide goggle,
Clown of our desiring one lifts the smock prying for trouble,
Up and into the secret divide and finds a cloth fool.

Loose long sleeved for concealing, pleading and winged
Mystery, the arms are empty of meaning, no oracle
Nor clue. Clown must tease, must tell more than a frill,
A fun woolly nose, or the limp stumps of a lackwit.

Nothing. So what. One craved love's yes no, kiss or grit,
Sleep clasping it, the cloth legs floppy with rapture.
Throw it then to bin or jumble. No, let be. We both are
Rags, riches, grin of a one unknown nature.

# Young Girl of Clacton

Here's a brass beehive, yellow rinse droned with eggs,
A queen in stupor, honey for the street corner.
While the cut hair writhes mourning on lino
Bees stagger from her mouth sipping for drugs.

Here's a tomb, gangrene  finger-smeared on lids,
Stones rolled away from sky-blue stare and flutter,
The great worm is hers to coax and flatter,
From under eye-shadow spring the funeral buds.

Here's a slot machine and the fun-fair witch
Styled for the coin in fringed rainbow mohair,
The caress of the net gloves leading nowhere,
The printed card is fortune's giggle and touch.

# A Lover

Kindle, scrabble in it, poke my log fire.
Do, my darling, though it fidgets, oh so irritates.
I hint, he ignores, does not budge, dubs me tease, liar.
Yes, he trowels in the wrong bulbs, seeds in wrong places,
Fumbles my pearl buttons, a lover's chance,
But shrinks from undoing,
Lazes in a daze all day switching telly sillies,
His help washing-up a daft clowning, so clumsily slow,
Drops the towel, stops to scratch an eyebrow.
All this crap, this caper slays us, slams the door.
While I despair, wither and must die,
Do, with a shut-eye kiss, a snare of riches,
All you can dare, and more.

# Recorded Delivery

A sharp ring. I harken, I crick neck softly sly
To pry out of a side window. Who comes, why
Or what. Someone dim idling by the front door.
A man, a dumb clot, in that flop hat, could be either.
The glass pane glistening a bright confusion.

A sharp knock. Maybe the dread mortgage to be sworn for
And signed. Or a rude refusal, a defiance, a threat.
Laundry, cash not paid, not mine. Or must serve on a doom jury.
My pulse tumbles. Today I cried in a dread disease of fury.
A smart double knock. I go, scribble, tear it apart.
Oh life, oh relief. He sends love, kisses and all all his heart.

# Wrong Number

My love my lord is cause of my heart's cramp,
My stammering pulse, and is gone from our damp bed-sitter.
My mouth dry, my tum a worry clutch in a sick sinking,
I loaf in this bald silence collapsing, craving for the ringing,
For the forgiving phone call from my life's darling.

I curl tense in deep sleep. The sudden bell rejoices me upright.
A voice smiles a rigmarole precise, vibrant;
'May we interest you in light, in Double Glazing.'
Undone, defeated I try dozing in the far forever.
Some time long after he is warm in my arms, the sun blazing.

## A Bench

A bench beside a murky canal, blind windows,
A warehouse, here the boss god stacks cash,
Rats chew on the banknotes of rubbishy dud ideas.
A flotilla of litter, of crumpled sighs, floats slowly.
Now urchins yelling, punching among black cinders.

Urchins snigger, hop, cackle, eyes roll up in mock grief.
Thumb and fingers prod, poke, tease, come closer. Spit jeers
With sneering treble laughter, with lip-smacking
Mimic agony of an adoring beyond belief.
We, you and I, on this metal bench weeping our goodbye,
Torn apart, tears glistening as they tumble.

# The Caravan

Ho there you caravan gaudy in two-colour
And bridal tin, you there in a winter's thumb-print
Of apple twigs on the sky's paper pallor,
My necessity must prove you eden innocent.

The smoke erect, stretch of washing in the smudged branches,
The hint and purpose in her thickening waist-line,
The mats shaken, the frayed angel guarding their fences
Sword against sin, and the only despair mine.

Bet on it, shirt and faith on them, on their rainbow
Box cradle, or accept the sick world has no return.
Now she stares for his homecoming, arms akimbo,
Yellow hair nagging the distance, her eyes bright with scorn.

# Chain Smoker

In my upstair child bed I fidgeted thrashed wildly,
My nightie up twisted in a flannel furious anxiety,
I bit, ripped, saliva the sheet, my head banging.
They wailed, the two of them, a harsh, a soft hate mumble.
The brat to blame, grumbled at it, a sigh and snort,
Half heard. Suppose he hit, kissed, killed. I hide, I tremble.

My child grief long laughed at, lost, a cig loading it deep under.
Strike match to cig. Grown, I loll sullen in a lone chill nylon.
Stub this red glow flat, flame another. Give it up. No, will not.
Elegance of fingers, lips hungry. Ponder. Then fill the wonder
        breath,
Seven lighters close by for life's ease, a trash of ash saucers.
Mama, Dad dead in battle, gone long into the clasp of lovers.
Stub one and light another, I follow them, crying out.

# Faces

Two dots, a blob below, gash under, all mock faces
Anywhere, in a cloth rag's twist and shadow,
In fold of an old coat flung down,
A forgotten duster roughed with the stale hours.
Faces side and full, grin, a groan, a kiss, frown,
A curtain fall hinting the secret of a sob.
My love living behind my eyes laughing at nothing,
My lost love mocking vanishing and still all my own.

# The Deck Chair

She is pregnant, the heels stamping her breath,
The sun hot with a head's unborn wrath.
Standing to a collapse and pang of sweat
She endured the two fists rippling in riot.

She sank into the deck-chair, thankful,
Relaxing in the blank of time, brimful
Of green air and the dithering gnats,
Canvas to grass where the notch fits.

She woke, the apron and the will ready
For routine chores, cardigan, kettle, bed.
But, Lord in Heaven, she cannot get up
Held fast by the chair's yawning lip.

She cannot rise up; now, forever
Tight swollen in the jaws of the deck-chair.
She struggles, whimpering, on and on
And alone. Oh why will nobody come?

# *Encounter*

Should one blown street forlorn in stone
Hold our two selves at some frail time,
As bubbles join and fall our loves might fall
Torn lightly down since love was known,
Pricked in our eyes beyond a breath's recall
On darkness once  my own.

And I should tremble, speechless and undone,
At this blind shade of love; amazed
As though dead Lazarus had come
Summoned before me out against the sun,
Bound hand and foot within the dazed
Endeavour that must hold him dumb,
And his beloved face
Wrapt in a napkin from the dark embrace.

## Sell-by Date

She is lost deeply in frayed years, in muddled debt,
Her life loose wobbling a melancholy, an odd doubt
Of ribald and cold hugs of darling lovers.
She born in a dim past, pleased proud and no blue lies.
Scorn her, she has dud nothing, or not much,
This dolt cannot add subtract multiply, plays silly.
This She is I, and you too who, claiming me with a touch,
Smiled into my back door and shut it.

# A Linen Line

The narrow white sheet strains on the linen line.
All shapes, sizes fluttering tugging weep in rain,
My loveless briefs pegged primly folded, my nothing bra,
The wet frilled petticoat simpering unworn,
The torn lace nobody's touch, socks stumbling to nowhere,
And jumble pyjams rinsed from a flop faint,
Rain wind insult, darken and defy me.
A lone cunning in my smiling folly.

On now. Toss of the double sheet pegged on a white breath,
The briefs blown free, petticoat a sweet truth.
Here are long-johns prancing high-kicking on twin limbs,
The lordly woolly vest opening wide arms.

# Man and Wheelbarrow

Rattle and squeal, old groggy wheelbarrow, come and go.
Stop. Fill it. Man loading grins at his mind's-eye potato
Breaking out of a black dot, a white weak belief,
Up to a hurrah and hallo of leaves and love-giving.
Man's dry mouth fills wet with the home thought of it.
So the pause, the lung's breath, a shovelful, another,
With dung to barrow, with the glad lift and on go.
This is the sweet man, mine, I his. Potato, I greet you.
Wheelbarrow, creaking old collapse, I salute you.
He so very nearly threw me and for his loaded lover.

# *Hanging Up Washing*

Vapour smoke of frost, half smear, drizzle there,
Wet air frost, house in a shroud, a soak, a numb trouble,
Rain a dazzle blotting out her why how or where.

She a dolt, a round the twist, nutter, heels soggy battered,
Knees a collapse, lugs out this basket of sorrows rinsed out,
Why peg out, hang out the wash, thickhead, of pain sodden
    tomorrows.

His rag pyjamas, woolly out at elbow, a vest for polish,
A peg-up a lover's pink shirt, pants once a rowdy shindy,
Fluff nightie, nylons, kisses, no never winners, wide spread
    for trash.

Why in drizzle, frost vapour, rain slanting torn despair,
Why struggle, peg up this rebus on linen line, this nonsense.
Puzzle too lost, go with a peg ready in hand and teeth
    to help her.

# Dandelion

Stop it, mower, mowing-machine cut that damn clatter,
Dandelions are script for the final and first god particle,
Sun in splinters and a singularity; leave them alone.

You too with the saw and chain death tackle,
Leave it alone; the white gash, groaning as it crashes,
Sighs with sin, leaves shuddering sunless, unredeemed, done for.

Answer, you there, what's to do, emerald stripes for spike heels
Aimed for, are they. But here's a sly secret, my fun whisper:
Roots of dandelion, yes they do, lurk deep below and undying.

# A Weed

I hate myself. Woman idle I groan giggles, suffer tum churnings
Of long-ago grief trash, stammer an amazed alarm
At what once my heel childishly smashed; so to a hangover harm
Left smouldering, to a clout hair-pulling, to sly cheatings,
To a bundle of damp fibs. I stole then and risked it.

A bonfire of it won't do. Rubbish in this ash a charred gold sandal,
Child's bonnet, beloved photo of somebody's old flame,
In smouldering sins the soft hiss and crackle of my lost name.
Okay, mine's the blame. But tell me now how out of this riddle
I gave you a weed in bud, and how we both laughed and kissed it.

# A Champagne Cork

Pulse of the fontanelle flutters as the cork explodes out.
Sometime this newborn will denounce, smite us in riot and far rot.

Out with spurt jet and shower in the rip-roaring age-coming
Soon vanishing cork and child will chill and condemn us dumb.

Cork bridal to gush pop out, fly out with white blossom,
　　a knife shared.
Cry wine soured, two knives twice to stab and be shunned.

Oh a keepsake. Cork rooted out from a dim junk drawer.
Rubbish it. No. All ours, dear love, with a lost kiss for saviour.

# *Egg*

Egg, double-domed, hidden amazement and my tryst,
This oval saffron circled in dense clarity
Egg, the crimson speck sparked in the first galaxy,
Laid on dawn rock in mist, mould, on thin twigs.
I bully you, brood on, boss, nag you in the long pause.
Out of air twist claws; fluff love feathers, comb red in greeting
Fun on fence, stutters, song. And you too run to meet me.
My hand holds Egg, a planet, palace, all promises.

## *Mouse*

Night quiet. The cat sat on the mat. Idle.
Young spotted tabitha, topaz gaze on the floor crack.
Faint bland odour of mouse. Will it. Come on out.
So out. Alert now, both on high haunches, paws up.
Ponder. Then cat's claw loads with a left hook, smack;
Mouse, a light-weight, delivers the right, the upper cut,
Leading with his chin, sneezed, and dazed whiskers.
A second wind, but game, coming up for more,
Tabitha floored him, down and out for the count.
But not. But rocking forward with a jab, the paw
Caught kitten-cat, fuddled her, shocked her.
Enough, stop to pat hit and miss. It's a draw.
Now cat's sheathed comfort sweet on her nose.
Mouse ambles to his hole, the home crack:
Praise and clap the champion.

## Tail on Fire

All this love stuff is a puzzle for trouble.
How cat dotes, near to toppling at skid angle
Shoving love's weight crazy against one's stockings,
Orange engine murmuring sweet nothings.

And once got going cannot check ardour,
The fool must rub harder, roam off further,
Must adore everybody everything with fever,
Must lean, plain daft, into the electric fire.

Tail in flames, on fire. Fire's erect flower,
Radio's red high torch, firework sparkler,
Love's pyre. Gale blowing, and cat bolts to window,
God in Heaven, what next must one endure.

Stench of singed adoration on fingers,
Damn, how a burnt tail stinks and angers,
Kisses in fur are for one's own reprisal,
This love business is a puzzle for trouble.

# Cat Nut

Nut my cat, my soul's one other self, a lifelong all mine,
Lies dying, topaz eyes wide with the last shine.
She dies, prick ears beg me to solve the sky riddle.
Oh why? I weep then, I her heart's double, kneel, caress her,
Her paw in my thumb and finger, I her handfast,
My falling hair folds our tangled silence.
So I tell her. No, it is ours only. And only with the kiss.
She ruckles, is content, is smilingly still.

# Two Dogs

She-dog Muckle, more than dying dark dog,
All four-footed life lit in wide eyes, in spry nose
And tongue, full force into mine a single glow gaze,
Loving, grieving, following on pad and claw
Into the evermore, wherever I happen to bid obedience.

Her clouded gaze now senses the edge of nothing,
Of black air and dares the galaxy. So plunge and leave me.
But never leave me. Muckle, I hold your paw,
And more. Our shut eyes clasp and tangle into one,
Shine together, adore the whole of all, smile, mingle.


A rescued dog, dog Ajax, Alsation plus mix of some other,
His the lush plume, the gay waving tail-wag,
The lavish coat two-toned of tan and ochre,
A comb defied, the rough span darling to my touch,
His gaze the beseeching of a lost lover.

Dog Ajax jumps in with a gift, the day's dump,
Spiked teeth white and wide on wood. Or log lump or bough,
Or a long length, or broken fencing. Chews, drops it,
Rolls on it over and over, belly up, paws in air.
How do I dare say Please, Thank you, kiss between his ears.
Alone, and rescued too, I will not shed tears
But linger by the window.

# A Cow

Timid, afraid, made curious, is brave, poor cow
Tugged two ways, and troubled. Flies around eyes, droppings
Hardening under dull trees. She dribbles.
Somewhere terror between turf, hooves, a staring gloom,
Cow groans a misery moo, cannot budge, broods.
Maybe she tries the wild head-on trample, stifle it.

I the threat, fright, the dreaded obstacle,
An oddity frolicking around in a wet field.
I am sorry, am silly, will strive to sweeten poor cow.
So stand, body flop easy, balanced in the long quiet,
Hands loose on thighs, a mind wise on air. She stares.
Now my nostrils blow puff breathing, sighing it.
Cow strolls slow, slower up to my heartbeat.
Close. The slobbering great tongue greets me,
Cow licks, lives, loves, kisses me.

# Sheep

Sheep topples over, trips over a tuft of grass,
Flat on back, her four hooves in air, she lies helpless.
Sheep strives in agony of struggle, then fades quiet.
Others sniff, nibble, gaze at pale sky, do nothing.
Sheep is topsy-turvy, eyes glazed, and learns to die.
Unless I am made aware, unless by chance I turn and dawdle by.


# A Goat

Goat high upright on hind legs, white, smiling,
Pleading oh do adore, admire me, bleating am I not amazing.
My horns scribbled, twisted wide by that sly Aaron
Scolding me to tiptoe a tall divinity in the sun.
My two hooves bent humble in supplication.
Here comes a lady primly mincing a sing-song and silk chic.
So to love her eye to eye I advance in love's subjection.
I bleat my primal choral in high hope, in delight.
Oh, she hollers, screams, she screams in a fainting flight,
In wild shock.

## A Hen

Fox circles, sniffs earth, smells a divine flavour.
Belly crawls. A shadow now, claws, scrabbles down under  wire.
He takes her. Snaps, takes my pet hen. Look. Feathers.

My grandpa died. Had tickled me with crazy card tricks,
With magic strings. My Mama left me then and I cried.
A goodbye to a someone with ring and a wet kiss.
A growl and a grumble of tyres took my teacher away.
Ambulance, aspirin, my head under a sour blanket.

Red and tawny, full-feathered, my sweet hen, a lover.
Once a battery-bald and dim eyed,
A heart wound deeper than these woes and all others.

# Red-Leg

Red-leg is spread lightly on seven eggs.
Not seen, but told so. No need whispering so clumsily,
Feathers dappled to obliterate all our fool chattering.

Name is Partridge. Once when seventy-five millions warmed to
    flame
She toppled in, dizzily squelched out, squealed her dyed legs
Red out of the sun's pool, preening her breast now for this long
    brooding.

Chosen, yes, angle with bricks and shed, twist of grass for cover,
Wall only from trucks, lorries, the rumble and traffic kill.
She, of a sudden, seven in tow, struts by. All now gone forever.
Left now with the broken egg-shells, the dent of a nest,
Her love spilling over.

# Albino Bird

Double-barrelled shot-guns on dread calendar days
Go crack bang and bang up to the damp haze,
Tumbled pheasants fall, their wide wings a whirligig,
A terror of sky scribbles denting the soft earth thud.
Kin to them, and I a pheasant, odd bird of luminous white
      feathers,
Am stunned low, must not dare fly, be plucked, burnt.
I shuffle under the odour of the car-shed, neck bent,
Tremble into a puddle of oil, of drip, stink and dross, hide.
Press breast to the mother, to the rubber tyre,
Then all guns gone. Soon I will fly, and high up, fly up higher
To dazzle my lamenting kin with white splendour.

# Walking By

Urgently wildly crazily walking by, why
Or who, tramp or trash, in jumble torn hand-outs,
Or is it sky-blue jeans faded mouldy in this haze,
Creature talking to self, gabble growling to himself, and so
      childish.

Walking by with murmuring, with plod swearing mutterings,
Now near and louder, and fuddled, striving, desperate
To define the clue, the one dazzling celestial riddle,
To solve, to tell it. But this our window is stiff-latched and shut.

# Old Lady

What's she up to, what's biting her? Mind gone batty
Maybe. Spidering out of the dawn door like that,
Grime dotted black in the pores of her neck,
A web of hair up and hair down fluffed on a knuckle.

And clothed backwards. Maroon cardigan on skin
No one but the eye of plastic buttons has seen.
A blouse next, flowering on time's buttocks,
Then the camisole where mirth has bent the hooks.

For the last, for the outward, for the street's glory,
Ribbon shoulder straps, a purl and plain woolly
Vest. She is off to Early Communion,
Slap into the double traffic to some vision
To kneel stark naked.

# *Adam*

Adam lay bound in her bond, his bladder at ease, spent,
Under his hair the five vowels and a divine lip grunt,
A gut stomach cacophony defiance the wife objects to,
She tastes the low sweetness and soft-entangled is asleep now.

His upright twice over urgency and her hip caught,
A marvel, an amaze, but nothing to shout about.
She pulls fruit, biting the half, from trees at sun dawn,
A stick and he plugs roots in a hole and lifts a stone.

Adam bound in her bond, sudden convulsed, shakes in fever,
Shudders, spies above in a leaf stir, python the strangle lover.
Death then the certainty, a new knowing; he gropes the sleep skins,
Binds them warm to loins, his throat dry terror with the first sin.

# Death of Adam

Vulture pecking me, stabs into this now nobody, my breath gone,
My eye up turned, slit smiling on a failed memory
Of wings never my own. Now rock-bound at sundown,
A cadaver pecked white, loved so neatly, this feast of me.

Sky vultures, sun thrown, a throng two four five, nine ten, scatter
Down, catapult in a canopy of a black intent,
Talons spread to slide down and in, wings wide in squabbles
Clap close, fold in on this violent rejoicing.

Was cold, bored. I begged for a carry-up to this hillside,
The end all, the call down to these god vultures, gliding
The high joy between beaks, the bare necks, I their pride's beloved,
The sky rinsed innocent. Now smiling I may learn to fly.

# God

Whoever, whatever, you the elusive big boss,
Listen, obey, twist undone those azure buttons off.
Toss the stony stars into the black hole. But not enough;

Strip the coat, fine size, the radiant, the red one,
With the fleecy lining, the pockets cirrus, nimbus.
I grope for his mountainous fingers, his handfast.

Why resist, refuse that shirt, that snowy vest,
I insist, tug, tease, grumble, win the unfair tussle.
Clothes in a heap. No, no naked divinity. But only air and air

# Satan

Holy one, true you fell. What knocked, stunned you silly.
Who bumped into you, pitched you out of Heaven and over.
Who or why or nobody. Solely your manic mood curiosity
And a bruised nose. So you spat on, mixed up the 'Yes, no, never',
Roared a thunder laughter to think up the roasting in Hell.
Then leaned over too far, toppled, tumbled, yelled and fell.
Down, oh down through the black air and you stand beside me.
Do I in sweat terror grip his hand, kiss him, or hide.

# A Grave

Lend me to myself to peer into my grave,
I see an eye wink and the wing feathers of a dove,
Ten tall lovers bending to whip and save.
I dig myself in deeper with nothing everything to prove.

# A Long Farewell

I forget what I had forgotten, so then to forget
My tangled my trembling, my own, my darling self,
For the smiling long farewell from that sweet man,
Be tossed down the time gulf, to a dark sun,
To the self speck, my crib, my sweet dadda, a smiling doll,
Back to the lost, to our secret, our sacred, soon then to resolve all.